D1231330

the Volunteer

CANDACE BLACK

Robert ———

Thank you again
for helping The Volunteer
become a book.

Candace

© 2003 by Candace Black
First Edition
Library of Congress Card Catalog Number: 2002117333
ISBN: 0-89823-217-1
Minnesota Voices Project Number 103, 2003
Cover designed by Julie Mader-Meersman. Interior designed by Renae Brandner.

The publication of *The Volunteer* has been made possible by generous grants from the
Jerome Foundation and the McKnight Foundation. Additional support has been
provided by the many contributing members of New Rivers Press.

For academic permission please contact Frederick T. Courtright at 908/537-7559 or
permdude@eclipse.net. For all other permissions contact The Copyright Clearance
Center at 978/750-8400 or info@copyright.com.

New Rivers Press is a nonprofit literary press associated with Minnesota State
University Moorhead.

Wayne Gudmundson, Director
Alan Davis, Senior Editor
        Managing Editor: Donna Carlson
        Work Study: Charane Wilson
        Honors Apprentice: Robyn Schuricht
        Editorial interns: Kristen Garaas-Johnson, Athena Gracyk, Bret Hoveskeland,
        Crystal Jensen, Jessie Johnson, Leslie Knudson, Carrie Olofson, Brett Ortler,
        Josh Smith, Kristen Tsetsi
Julie Mader-Meersman, Design and Production Director
        Design Assistants: Erin Bieri, Renae Brandner, Shannon Tomac
        Photography Assistant: Rachel Broer
        Web Site Development: Timothy Litt
        MSUM Student Technology Team: John Jeppson, Bo Vargas
Nancy Edmonds Hanson, Promotions Manager
Marlane Sanderson, Business Manager
        Assistant Business Manager: Andy Peeters

Printed in Canada

New Rivers Press
c/o MSUM
1104 7th Avenue South
Moorhead, MN 56563
www.newriverspress.com

for Rick

and for
Keenan and Lewis

ACKNOWLEDGEMENTS

The following poems, some in slightly different form, first appeared in
these publications:

ART/Life: "Open Pasture"
Chariton Review: "Safe Passage"
Collage: "Osprey," "Save the Wishbone"
Graham House Review: "Laundry"
Great River Review: "Insomnia"
Gulf Stream Magazine: "Clearing," "The Lap Swimmer"
Folio: "St. Francis, Feeding the Sparrows," "Tornado Dreams"
Intro 10: "Wind Damage"
Iowa Woman: "Chickadees in the Hawthorn Tree," "Gold Horse, Brown Horse"
The Nebraska Review: "Kites, All For Keenan"
Passages North: "Quilts"
The Pennsylvania Review: "The Volunteer"
The Pharos: "Vigil"
Piedmont Literary Review: "Desert Plants"
Prism: "Below the High-Water Mark, with Gannon and Kyran"
Quarterly West: "Wedding Portrait: The Mother of the Bride"
Red Weather: "The Woman with the Pumpkin Head"
The Seattle Review: "Giving Blood," "On the Coast"
The Slackwater Review: "Arthur, in Your Letters," "For Luck's Sake"
Smackwarm: "False Spring," "Harvest," "Turkish Print Dream"(under the
    title "While You Were Gone")
Sport Literate: "Track Meets"
Sunrust: "Long Distance" (under the title "Bad News")
Tar River Poetry: "The Doctor Loses Three Patients in as Many Days"
Three Rivers Poetry Journal: "Postpartum: Shantung Province," "Three
    Carnations" (under the title "A Gift")
Visions-International: "Talisman"
Willow Springs: "Where Blood Collects"
Yarrow: "The Mauling"

I want to thank The Loft and The McKnight Foundation for a Loft-McKnight
Award of 1988, and SASE/The Jerome Foundation for a 1998 Fellowship.
I am also very grateful to The Ragdale Foundation for the time and space
that helped me write several of the poems in this book.

Contents

1.

2.

1

GIVING BLOOD

All those years I believed veins
blue rivers, only to find it true.
In lab, the cat's pumped
full of latex, it was easy to tell
them from nerves, tight ganglia.
Mine taught me the posture of death.
She clawed the gas, back arched.
Porcelain teeth we rang
with probes guarded the tongue, frozen
and pink like a Moslem tidbit.

My own veins grew skittish,
jumped away from needles to expose
bone. Bruises were violent
then green. One morning we cut
away fat, found the twin horns
bulging with kittens.

Even now I can't trust
this tearose stain on white tissue.
Somewhere in my body
a cave must be blooming, a steady dance
to the season it knows
like my name, like my heartbeat.
Lulled by narcotic iris,
the hammering at the temple
is not our pulse, only the echo
of one we listened for in the dark.
Long ago, our ears small petals.

For Luck's Sake

for Douglas

A woman doesn't name her child.
For six years the air's too full
of spirits eager for mischief.
This-One-Always-Cries will grow up knowing
the value of the silent word.

In the same way, your life is bordered
by what you do not name. With the ill
it's tumor: the air's too full
of fear, eyes promise time and hands
coax away pain. With us, it's love.

A woman doesn't name the child
she may never have. That word rides quiet
between the ribs, on the tips
of our fingers, always asking for a tongue
we haven't strength to give.

OSPREY

for Mark

Don't we always love
the wild? The snowy underbelly,
the wingtips that flutter
with each change of current,
your fingers so light I haven't memory
of their touch.
That morning
socked in with fog, I wanted
to trap it or hover there with it
at least
before the last steep dive
but you said, *Let it go*.
And don't we regret it in dreams
of two dead trees,
the irrigation canal, the winter
cry of the hunt.

THAT OLD ROLLERCOASTER

When you buy your ticket
at the invisible booth, and yes,
we all buy tickets here, you don't feel
his windfingers fleecing you of everything
sane. You close your ears
to the silent chorus that screams
Turn back.
Only your past
keeps you in your seat.
Yes, this is it, love,
or the ride there. And when you think
it's over, you step to an empty ribcage
convinced it will be tamer
next time. What you don't know,
what we never see, is the line of pure voice
singing through the curves.

Quilts

My grandmother was the center
of a trinity. She understood
the alliance of sisters. This was the logic

behind her gifts: afghans
knit in sequence, matching robes,
dress yokes of complex crochet.

Because she thought hard
about color, worked her dreams into each
stitch, we knew them as our own,

yet part of a piece. It made sense,
then, the day she unpacked three quilts
and told me to choose: Lemon Star,

Dresden Plate, Double Wedding-Ring.
My hands traced the edges
of Depression cloth faded to pastels.

Esther, the great-grandmother
from photographs, was there and I knew this choice
mattered: the youngest

trusted first, the heirloom mine forever.
Autumn tells me I was right
to resist the entwined climb

of rings, the conforming scallops.
I need eight-pointed stars
reaching out to all

directions, the hands of those dead
women around me at night,
the love of generations making its own heat.

The Woman with a Pumpkin Head

wears a sweater stuffed with leaves.
Her smile is pert, but crows
hear the dry wilt of her back.
You think she'd be miserable
out there in weather like this, but no,
even at night she sits
holding in her lap
a puddle of yellow luck.

Wind Damage

No sun. Weather spits
through on its way east,
forcing you indoors to the man
you'll winter with. Look him over
with an eye for time—it's come to that.
Tell him of men loved who died
early: Grandpa, a name with your mother's
face, Byron shot in Korea,
your only uncle dead at forty-six.

Point out the exceptions. Your dad,
approaching fifty, begins to breathe
easy. Be sure to mention Paul,
the great-uncle who hung on. His wife,
Mildred, swallowed salvation for him
and later—the priest gone—tried to kiss grace
past his startled lips. Her jealousy
of something vague as cancer, the secret
pride of keeping her vow longest
in a family of widows.

Tell him the blue spruce this morning
was only the start: eventually
barer, hungry arms will crack
through his dream, embrace him
in a way you never can. There are women
in trees who, rather than lose
one branch to a stranger wind,
let go and fall
toward whatever promise ground provides.

LAUNDRY

Think of the men you've left:
their assorted sizes
as you pile colors into mounds,
decide which can't be
stopped from bleeding. Check pockets,
but men are careful
at this age. Hands feel for damp
in socks, smooth the baggy
pouch of briefs. Stains
of younger brothers, Daddy's nylon
boxers, the ex-lover who went without.

Why do this? Clothes
have no new secrets, no clues
to the man inside. Try them on.
Feel his thigh around yours,
fold the sleeves to your breast,
say *his hands cover me*. Celebrate
the bleach that kills his salt,
leave your own in the crotch and collar.
It will bring him back
like a ticket.

False Spring

In another home I'd be victim
to the season. Orchards of almond
blossoming white, pollen drifts
behind limited vision.
Here, occasional foolish trees
dare a late snow, set out
their own lace. The sun
invites belief. Like robins, I steal
mud for daubing a new life.

General John Bidwell knew
what he was doing: hardwoods
for shade, fruit trees for sustenance.
Named the largest after an English friend.
Twice the same week loves call
from years away. We talk
of marriage, I listen for the unspoken,
but they seem only envious
of such guarantee.

It is Friday and morning's winter
melts into new grass. Hooker Oak
is dead: laid down
with such a thud birds this far north
started into sky. One man left
to call, the one I wanted most.
He wades through rice, checking levees,
indifferent to the air
of the red-winged blackbird.

BELOW THE HIGH-WATER MARK, WITH GANNON AND KYRAN

Early spring, after dinner,
we all walk to the far dock.
I've never known the lake
this low. Not like summer,
when snowmelt covers
our steps. You show me
where to look for shells
under driftwood. I never find
one on my own, but you both know water
and its secret places. My pockets
bulge. Above us, Red explores
the cliff. He's a good dog. Swallows
bank against glare and dip
out of range before we can say for sure,
Rough-Winged. On the dock,
you teach me to spot fish: don't
look for the dimple, look out
to Goose Island, or beyond, to Angel Point
and there, on your left, the splash,
the growing circle. Before sunset
you head home to bed. I'll follow
later, reading the maps
ice left on rocks. I'll stop at
the gift of your days, the cache
of shell and flat skipper.

Chickadees in the Hawthorn Tree

Seed on a tray remains
untouched, those black-capped
acrobats enjoying
their tussle with dark fruit.
Mid-August, the heavy
green silence of afternoon heat broken
only by a raucous indigo
arrow gliding from tree to fence,
to tree again. The jay
claims this yard. Lettuce
bolts but stays sweet. During winter
we will be fed by what grows
today. The pantry holds
applesauce in quart jars, dark treasure
pots of blackberry jam, chutney,
pickled beets, apple butter.
In those wet dull months, hungry
for this elusive and brief
season, we'll watch
the feeder: the flash of migratory
birds, the dependable colors
of old friends.

WEDDING PORTRAIT: THE MOTHER OF THE BRIDE

after a photograph by John Cohen

I've taken care of everything.
Thanks to me, this daughter
wears white. The eye shines brightest
before the vows are spoken.
And tonight! Who but me
has thought to lay the corn husk
doll beneath the bed?

Let the poor girl
admire her gloved hands.
After tonight she'll never touch
satin again. Only goat dung,
only blood: a chicken's,
a child's, her own.

Harvest

On a dark road leaves race toward
headlights like children
running home. We've made it
this far. To the dying
of the year, still whole.
Now is when trees give up, silver
maple turns in to itself. Only juncos
dare wind at the feeder. We turn in
to ourselves and dare what private
demons we carry. Mine is harvest.
Contrary to weather, I must fight
the fullness of autumn, struggle with my own wish
for a seed to carry through winter.
This bearing down of seasons makes me strong.

It's a hard time, when air
becomes something to be wrestled.
Let me take that for you, let me breathe
when you can't, calm as the resting branch.
My hand in yours means time: years
stretch out like a river
heading west, alive with moon from a night's
promise of frost.

I've hung corn and wheat
on the door. They mean hospitality:
the home we're building
will be Pocatello or Blackfoot, Archer
and Johnson, all the towns
we're part of. We'll become the lives we touch,
the ones we start by loving each other.
In the end, I'll close your eyes
if I have to. Let me kiss back all the life
you've given, hold you
beyond the point where touch is what matters,
my voice leading you home, and gone.

Turkish Print Dream

While you were gone
the woman you think of
as yours slept. The man
hiding in the lilac
approached the window, open

during your absence. He released
her ankles from their dreamless chase
and now, returned home, you feel her leaving.
Beyond her still body, a Turk
has nearly made the gate. Guards become suspicious

within the turquoise city. You become
one guard, powerless to move
beyond your crimson jacket, the gold lance,
certain your wife lies asleep
in the rogue's bag.

How to account for this distance,
the sudden growth of hollyhocks
in the garden, the stranger
holding your body whose mouth
stings like money? You'd kill

for the chance to talk with her
again. But you are frozen ten yards
from the gates, praying to Allah
the tower alarm does not sound, praying the woman
sleeping on your back won't stir.

CLEARING

1.

A man and a woman work
together, clearing

the garden after the first hard frost.
Corn whispers

sharp intrigue, but they do not
hear. They survey a ruined

kingdom: twisted crookneck,
tomatoes caged grotesque.

2.

Berries need a blanket
of straw, canes need to be cut back.

The last bees dust
the sunflower. Hail the brassica

finally thriving! Welcome the humble
finch. Soon it will be

the garden's only color.
Head's blood against snow.

3.

In the coming months, the woman
may grow dark with winter.

Her belly swells
taut. At night

the man rests his hands
upon her skin. He feels the change

inside her, the ground
being turned.

The Lap Swimmer

She stepped into water and began
swimming. What surrounded her
felt solid, her hands shovels
to move aside so many
fathoms of light.
Lulled by the gradual
descent to aquamarine, the slick
algae starting its cling to walls,
she saw herself growing old
there. The lover she dreamed once
swam before her, all thrash
and struggle in deeper water, in calmer
moments glinting copper,
always within and just out of
her reach. She did not stop.
Her arms cast for still more, the circle
of eternity flashing
gold on her left hand, an irresistible
lure in such clear water.

ARTHUR, IN YOUR LETTERS

you speak
of owls and hawks, predators
I never see at home, in the same
great flyway as you. Too many
houses, perhaps. The wind
blows only sparrows
to our feeder and you know
how they are—all buff and brown,
streaked, female or immature—yet each
so full of brash humility
the species becomes unimportant; only
its being there, head cocked,
counts; only that instant of trust
through glass counts.

We'd made the trip giving
thanks, grateful for a good marriage,
work, those migrating geese, a river,
hills of harvested corn, and friends.
Surely our prayers were heard
that night as we stood in the dark
street, listening to the owl,
the galaxy extended above us.

OPEN PASTURE

after a photograph by Roger Pfingston

For years you wanted to take
this photograph yourself:
two horses in snow.
We drove back
roads in search of the calico pony
you insisted would be there.
And now, given to impulse, a friend
visits, gives you
this Midwest pastoral: the black
barbed wire of the foreground
repeated on the stallion's rump,
his hoof poised, with more
grace than we possess, above his winter
shadow. The mare leads
as they graze
their way toward the break
in the sway-backed fence.

Safe Passage

Last winter's birds
have not returned. I want to blame
mild weather.
Duped lilacs have begun
to play their hand. The lawn is spongy
wet green. What need of us
have sparrows, when seed lies exposed
on bare ground? The sunflower head
is full, no flicker
lording it over the smaller birds.
I want to blame tall pines
across the street, dense and safe.
My trees are always playgrounds,
never home. Nesting birds are visited
graces: I must want them too much,
a mark of favor from those I can't help
but love.

       I spent lunches
watching for the white-crowned sparrow.
I was never sure: the glass
wavered just where he was, the juncos
bullied him away before I got a good look.
My one success: the house finch
I'd call down from the neighbor's
tree, to the phone lines
to the fence, to the juniper,
elm, and finally the feeder.
He'd eat, question, and I'd promise
Safe passage as long as I live,
winter flag, trusting heart.

For Bob: A Drive through the Pintlars to Butte

Surely we deserved that day,
the clouds breaking after a week
of fog, deserved fields reaching out
into a stubbled January and always,
some range to the south
or west. In Philipsburg we tried
reciting poems but couldn't, the gray
there claimed by waxwings. *Bohemians*
like us, we said. How did we explain
Anaconda, the stack
empty of profit
as ever? When your plane took off
how small the rest of us seemed: trucks
hauling copper out of Berkeley Pit,
trees turning make-believe, mountains
and rivers flattened of all relief. You flew
away. I drove home, both of us leaving
Opportunity behind, forever advertised
and hidden from the road.

LONG DISTANCE

Bad news comes by phone.
An interruptive ring, a welcome
voice, then the eternity
when my heart stops, and starts
again as I walk, blind, as far
as the twisted cord, modern
umbilical between mother and daughter, reaches.
I discover the filthy
grout of kitchen tile or the bedspread's
intricate weave, holding on
to detail while the enormous fact
of tragedy—Gonga's stroke,
all the inoperable cancers—washes me
out to sea.

I was home alone
when my uncle died. I memorized irrelevant
messages on tiny cells of cork
while my aunt reported: plane crash,
dead, tell your parents. Sixteen years later,
I know I did it wrong. Should have talked
to my dad, should have warned
I have bad news, but I needed
my mother's voice and when I heard it
I started sobbing, blurted out *Jack's dead*
and set her adrift, without her brother.

Of course we do it wrong. Even the expected
deaths come as a shock, no matter
how often we rehearse a final
illness or freak accident, the Intensive Care
vigil of movies. The last-minute
flight west will always take too long.
No amount of imagination
can understand *never, forever*, the casket
sealed and lowered into that precise
hole. Nothing prepares us
for the pain that becomes congenital: a condition
we live with, a limp we grow used to,
a scar others hardly notice.

THREE CARNATIONS

Kathryn died yesterday, the youngest of three
sisters. According to the family,
she was the old woman I'd grow into.
Carol would be Aunt Alice, Marilyn our grandma.
I will be no one now.
On the sill above my desk,
a small branch grows in a clear jar.
Windblown, it forgives
by leafing out anyway, forks jagged
against an empty backdrop of sky.

Everything seems to forgive
our impatience for the season's change.
The pussywillow's fur
dotted with pollen. The geranium
in bloom. Even the crow coughs a blessing
as I work out back,
spreading compost or raking mulched leaves.
Last week my husband gave me
three carnations. The shredded edges open
and we taste clove in our dreams.

The lilac above me lives.
Is it too much to hope
pale green fleur-de-lis will flower, white,
heavy with scent? Kathryn's heart
gave out. A year ago she announced
she was dying, but no one
believed her. I believe the light that fills
my window later and later each day,
the slow shift of earth. I cup
my hands in the garden and inhale
the peppered scent of dirt.

St. Francis, Feeding the Sparrows

We each wear the earth's
colors. Gray
of cobwebs and morning
fog. Your feathers,
my cowl. Fields
newly plowed. Umber. We rejoice
together over the world's
gleanings, the dusty
sunlight of afternoons. My cowl.
And isn't daybreak the quiet
treasure, as the town's
chimneys sift
silver. Your feathers.
                            Yes,
I've brought your crusts
of bread. Such bold eyes of slate.
Each day I hear
your trusting orison. Little
shy one, come closer.
Your feathers. For you,
making the longer journey of faith,
a blessing.

On the Coast

for Dick

When we came to the end
of the river: confusion. Sky
had risen to meet us, or was it the arc

of water into low gray clouds?
We strolled all afternoon. The ring-bills
mocked our generous lunch

until we tossed it to them, the bread
assuming a brief, curious birdlife,
flying off in two directions.

Direction. We had not known the river's
name until you spoke it, wandered lost until
you pronounced the ocean Scottish,

the unseen sun north-west.
That was all there was time for.
We turned for home, walking

backward, waving long past the yellow
smudge of you waved back, the spray
misting our eyes, the gulls mewling lonely.

2

Postpartum: Shantung Province

Rice from the flooded terrace
cannot touch my lips.
The fish that flashes
silver continues upstream
as do the duck
and goose, free to browse watery
roots. The mother
of my husband sets the plate
before me: chicken—that land
loving bird—again, red peppers,
carrots brilliant as a sunset.
To quench my thirst
she gives me boiled water, barely
cooled. When she leaves
the room I stand at the window,
knowing that to open it, even to sniff
the fragrant quince, would bring
bad luck to my sleeping
child. My flow has not
stopped, my hair hangs lank
and unwashed. No wonder
my husband finds excuses to sleep
in the other room.

KITES, ALL FOR KEENAN

1. Carp

Black gills and wild
yellow eyes proclaimed your birth
to the neighbors. We grew
used to it, as our lives
changed to welcome you, and then noticed it
gone: swept over the Cascades
during the big storm.

2. Against the Sun

Out for a drive and looking
west we saw a black witch riding
her bucking broom. The road
turned and we saw a broken box
kite. Remember this.

3. Outside the Baby's Window

The morning glory
leaf, stained with decay and turned
in on itself, twirls in the dawn's
half-light on the vine that chokes
the rose bush every summer.

4. Tri-Colored

Dancing above us
the way swallows do, banked
roll and deathless
plunge, three diamonds
magically fused in the primary
colors. Tied to this
earth by the slightest of threads,
its tails write our names
in the wind's code.

The Volunteer

We've learned
not to question such obvious
gifts. The sprawling
vine snaking out
from the compost's heat
has declared itself
pumpkin: yellow trumpet
blossoms, prickly leaves, hard
green globes.
And it doesn't matter
if it survives
the summer. It doesn't
matter if November
comes and squash blaze
gold in the overgrown
lawn. We've already been judged
worthy. The gift
is in being chosen.
Like that afternoon I woke
and, nearly dreaming,
saw two tanagers brilliant
against the dark
green of the pine. I only knew
I had been blessed.

GOLD HORSE, BROWN HORSE

In the pasture behind
the house, an island of berries
ripens in the summer
heat. They will grow
plump, darker than garnets, then shrivel
away, or rotting, fall
to the brambles, tasted only by birds,
field mice. Two horses graze
here. They watch from a distance as you
whistle, their ears shifting with each
variation. One morning they reward
you and stand at the fence, flies
clinging to the moist corners
of their eyes. They know
how to take the offered
apple, even from a child's hand. Brownie
shies from the gold one. She comes
only when he moves on, and then
with hesitation. You stroke her forehead's
blaze, give her your palm to smell,
to nuzzle. Late August,
two horses rolling in the afternoon dust.

TALISMAN

after a photograph by John Cohen

She walks with purpose,
home from the market. One stalk
of corn to shake at the road
ahead, another in her pack,
wedged between next year's seed
and her youngest son.
She wouldn't say
which means more: one grain
from the cob of her body
or a rocky patch of tilled chance.

This year's *quipu* will tell
the harvest. Knotted strings
keep history. Not this woman.

VIGIL

The seasonal croup had filled the ward
with children struggling for air,
telltale barks in foggy tents. I lived

in the reclining chair
next to Keenan's caged crib, slipping
my hand beneath the plastic

to hold his into sleep, the electronic
blip of a baby's heart
monitor our erratic lullabye.

When the nurses floated in at 4:00
they *were* angels: silently
efficient as they charted fever and liquid

intake, changed soggy
sheets while I held the mask of therapeutic
vapor to my son's face and crooned

him calm. I believed his daily
improvement, but I could not leave him.
My breath was tied to his, each fit

of coughing jolting me
awake. I stayed three days underwater,
surfacing on our way home

to find it irreversibly autumn, leaves
fallen and crackling underfoot.

CARVING

for Marcie

Thawed, resting on the counter, the chicken
looks almost childlike: knees
flexed against the body, goose-fleshed
in the winter kitchen. I sharpen the knife
and think of my son, weeks old,
sleeping upstairs. College anatomy
taught me where to look
for the joint, cartilage between
bone and bone. The back
breaks. My breasts
burn, ready to let down, and I'm forcing
the knife now, stripping
skin away, forcing myself
to finish because the family must eat,
willing the baby awake
so I can wash blood
clots from my hands, gather
his body to me, and convince myself
of his wholeness.

OVERNIGHT

Arthritic branches swell
into leaves: pale green
flags of maple, the blushing
ensign of crabapple.

Grass competes with the temporary
violet for the treasured
soil of sidewalk cracks as yet unclaimed
by ants, those workers who bring the cold

air of underground to light.
Birds negotiate for territory.
Rusty-hinged crow, liquid
cardinal, self-conscious robin.

The constellations shift
and lovers stray beyond a late
sunset. Rhubarb unfurl.
Raspberries—only fuzzy suggestions

yesterday—reach
toward the rendezvous of blossom
and bee. Indoors, lives and tempers
quicken with imperatives: the ritual

exchange of storm pane and screen, comforters
shucked for the season, winter gear
stowed, summer clothes rediscovered.
Our firstborn holds his urine, the baby

sleeps through. You and I sleep angry
until one fits into the curve
of the other's back, declaring,
overnight, an unspoken truce.

SAVE THE WISHBONE

So much to hope for.
You settle for things working out
the way they should, wind up
with one more brittle arm that,
with all the others, piles up
in the chest. The sharp edges poke
through sometimes, when you sigh.

I wish for the time between:
the empty arc of all wishbones,
light and darkness and when they change,
the times we know we still
have love. It is somewhere behind
our eyelids with trust and the dark.

JANUARY REQUIEM

This is what I saw, Ed, the day
you buried your oldest child: clear
skies with traces
of mares' tails, skies so blue
that Keenan, *my* firstborn, told me
spring must be coming. I saw
stern saints line the church
walls, their Baroque colors dimmed
then flooded with light
as those clouds flicked
the sun. I saw the church
filled with boys like your Edjie: faces
struggling with the required pose
of tough, eyes bruised
with the first loss of a friend. Some were not
ashamed to cry, as Edjie would not have been,
as you were not ashamed to walk,
blind with grief, behind his coffin.
I saw that day the road, the winter
fields. Saw my sons again and knew how close
to the surface terror stays.

That spring
eventually comes can't bring much
comfort. Either the months roll
over us or we stumble through the constant
calendar, but winter does swell the river
while trees renew themselves and birds return.
By then you will be no longer numb. Feeling too much,
perhaps. Too aware of sap rising, days stretching
toward the solstice, the diploma
never to be awarded.
I saw that winter day the loneliness
of mourning, the helplessness of friends.
My eyes are open now.
I can never not see again.

Insomnia

1.

What kind of woman
are you, complaining
when the moon keeps you
awake?

2.

At the convention of dreams
a man steps to the podium.
My esteemed colleagues,
he begins. *My esteemed colleagues,*
and takes his life.

3.

It's been so long since I slept
through the night
that I dream in the still
hours, between drink
of water and child's moan,
list of tomorrow.

4.

The first
bird claims the day
at 3:45.

Tornado Dreams

Always glass. In one dream
it's a sliding door.
In another, the entire store front.
Always glass that lets me

notice the suddenly green
cobbled sky, the swirling core
on the hunt.
Always glass that will be

sucked out, a glittering scream,
or punched in by the twister's roar.
In the worst, that wakes me with the blunt
thud of heartbeat,

Lewis toddles just beyond reach.
I lunge across the floor
and grab him safe, but whipping trees taunt
my attempts at speed,

the way I herd Keenan under the safest beam.
My feet trudge in a war
with themselves. Always glass that's caught
by equal strengths: the menace seen

and the terror beneath
the surface. I know that impulse to let go and soar
on panic's rush. It's easy to want
oblivion. Like glass I'm framed, but between

children, doing my brittle best, a thin
seam holding, holding. Nothing more.

THE DOCTOR LOSES THREE PATIENTS IN AS MANY DAYS

for Tom

Small matter they were old,
their hearts too weak
for another season of breath.
The doctor sleeps
when he can, despite the hoarse
rattle and straight line
weaving his dreams together.

His garden is sown in even
rows. He loses himself
among the tendrils and runners
pulsing green. Squash swell
like fingers, the snowpeas
in their pale curves, embryonic.

And we are all growing
toward decay—the garden,
the small yellow bird
darting in the tree, the many
hearts the doctor will not save.
Small wonder we praise
the child, who knows the words

for *ball, butterfly.*
Who sees his father in all
bearded men and sleeps
through the night, trusting
two faces. The doctor
learns to trust each symptom,

none, to usher the dying.
He sleeps when he can.

LIES

Just how much do we want
him to know? When I saw Keenan
flip off the nextdoor kids I felt that familiar
see-saw of wonder and woe.

I didn't know his five-year-old
fingers could do that, didn't know that gesture
looked just as defiant on his twig
limbs. I told my son

it meant a word so hurtful and mean
I didn't want to say it
myself, and tasted the salt
of half-truth. Hardened as we are,

it still hurts to receive that word's
slap. But it feels so good and comes out
so easy, that hissing fricative
thudding into the hard

consonant of *k*. There's nothing
like English for swearing, those goddamned
Anglo-Saxon clots of sound
hurled like rocks. But there's time

for learning that. He still lies
purely, holding on to his claim
of a single piece of gum
while five wrappers litter the counter,

his cheek bulging like his baseball
dream. Soon enough,
the lies of omission, the fine
art of never volunteering

more than necessary, filtering.
That's how children and parents
survive: we all know more
than we let on, hold back what will get us

in trouble, what we think
they're not ready to know.

Training Wheels

My father called it clutch time,
those weeks after I got my license,
when I was on call
for any errand. I lived in the delicate
tension of first gear: left foot
releasing while the right bore down.
A balance. A listening with the muscles
of my leg. I'd stop on deserted inclines,
empty straightaways, to test
myself. Stopping and starting. Stopping
and starting. My body knows
that dance so well I still,
driving the occasional
automatic, stab for the clutch
at sudden stops.

I watch my son careen
down the walk on his bike,
body tense with fear and studied
ease, training wheels
correcting like an angel's wings
any radical shift from the middle way.
We're supposed to shorten them
each week until he trusts
his inner ear. We're supposed
to remove them and stand back,
knowing he'll fall, and fall again.
The way my dad gave me the keys
and went inside, listening to the throttle
whine to the stop sign
and drive away.

A Christmas Card

Above us, people fly to either coast
for the holiday, huge jets
reduced to a steady blinking we mistake,
at first, for stars. Those travelers,
racing beneath the waxing moon, look down
and see scattered islands
of light. They think of the dark
heartland, mid-America,
centered and safe. And tonight,
for once, they're right. Yard lights
anchor farms afloat on the rolling plains,
bluemilk snow lapping
against barns and fence posts. Roof lines
defined by twinkling color,
evergreens filling front windows
with anticipation—it all says welcome,
and warmth, and good care.
We're driving through its secret,
sleeping heart, quintessential family
of four in our American-made import, cargo space
packed with gifts. The kids
aren't whining and we are happy,
singing along with a great oldies station, the promised
gas and food
nine miles ahead and there,
over the river and through the woods,
two days away, Christmas.

Radar

I've seen it in action.
We'd met for lunch,
the country mouse of her
come to the city, children in tow,

and all her wires were bristling:
alert for culture, big trucks,
construction, things of interest, street signs
for the known route

back home. The kids had eaten
and when her youngest wanted to use
the bathroom alone
she tried so hard to be casual.

Came back to the table and chatted
while her eyes danced
to every adult bussing dishes. Bolted,
mid-sentence, and ran

for the hallway. Returned with a teary
boy too small to push the door
open, whose call she'd felt
more than heard. She says

she tries to turn it off: practice
for the life ahead
when they move out of range,
the rapid heartbeat

of their insistent blink
offscreen. She'll find out
how deep it goes,
throbbing so long next to her own

pulse they merge,
until the odd crisis flares
it back into the familiar rhythm
defining her days.

Desert Plants

for Jimmy

1. Agave

Your letter arrives
bearing the stamp of agave.
Surely you remember the century
plant in front of our house.
In my dreams it bloomed for us
our first conscious year
in the high desert. That spring
we buried our dog.
Could we still find its small grave?

2. Barrel Cactus

When lost
remember its curve to the south.
It will survive,
stronger than drought or frost.

3. Beavertail Cactus

Whoever named this was homesick
for an excess of water
trapped behind log-jams.
Warty growths along the spine
offer fruit, often edible.
Later, hunger eased,
hands will burn in a hell
of red ants and velvet
no animal ever thought of.

4. Saguaro

They had never seen anything
like it in that land
tinted penitential and ash,
arms reaching
toward the God they felt sure
no longer watched their progress.
They rested in its shade.

Her Last Trip to Hawaii

We have photos
of earlier visits: with parents, with daughters,
draped with leis at the Don Ho show,
sunbathing on Waikiki, raising the tropical
cocktail in a cheery salute. She loved
the islands. Loved the warm water, the palette of green,
loved the fact of vacation
soaking into her skin with every eventual
melanoma.

That's not what killed her.
When her kidneys and heart gave up
we were left with ashes
and indecision. Three years later,
we're ready to let her go.

A daughter travels west through time and light.
She holds her mother's ashes
before the coarse grains sift
into salt water. No tears, no ceremony.
A casual cascade over the side
of the outrigger. A secret deposit
during a snorkling session.
Anywhere lovely and warm.

It may take another lifetime
before one atom of her existence
travels this far to bless us
in a single drop of rain. It could be
tomorrow.

THE MAULING

for Kim Eberly

You knew all the rules
only to ignore caution.
Summer, tent pitched
near the creek—the last stars
of a dream weekend. When your pulse
sounded that sure it helped you
forget a darker heartbeat, out
in the night, the animal
rage of finding you in its path to food.

Once you spoke of dying, wanting
to be destroyed by what you loved.
When they found your body
it was not romantic, not even the usual
tragedy we who live in that country
dread, but expect, each year. Call it careless
justice: the girl killed only
for being with you, you dying for the brother
attacked the year before.

Bear brother. Brother. Bear.

WHERE BLOOD COLLECTS

Hollows. Recesses.
The crease of the left elbow,
where a needle slips
in with a small sting
while a doctor explains
the procedure. Between tendons
of the right hand, two blue cords
rise out of the shunt's yellow
stain while the ulnar malleolus juts
like an island
surrounded by a rosy sea: twenty minutes
trying to establish an IV line, the veins
run for cover in the frigid
cath lab, the carpal tunnel
too narrow.

Blood meanders
until it meets resistance. The eggplant
on my thigh drifts
ever down, its leading edge perfect
as fronts on a TV weather map.
Blue-green border loyal to gravity,
interior a cauldron
around the catheter's puncture
site, boiling a jam
of raspberry or grape.
Hematoma. We use soft vowels
when we name the body's response
to trauma. Even everyday violence,
the chair's sharp corner,
forgotten
until a dark witness rises
to testify.

The Aftershadow of Trees

Autumn storm.
Sumac, poplar, ornamental
crab, maple. The wind
spreads their leaves' reverse
image on the ground below: a shadow
of flame, pale gold.
The storm scrapes our city clean. The river
full and fast, I walk past
the widow's house, the window begonia
blooming into an empty room.

For the Second Time, I Dream My Death

Unlike my standard anxiety
dream—the looming storm,

a child gone
missing—I stayed in this one

until the end. My point of view
kept shifting. Watching from a distance

my car, stuck in reverse, take
the wrong turn. Meeting my husband's

quizzical glance as he drives past.
Watching the car spin on snowpack

over the embankment. Looking toward sky
as the car sinks into black

water, heart pounding me awake
after the last light goes.

It felt like years ago
when I kept diving into a dream

wave that swelled into a *tsunami*.
I could never reach

the surface, my lungs exploding
as I struggled through

a mountain of surge
toward the sweetest air.

Track Meets

for the distance mothers

We settle on tiers
of aluminum, shading our faces
to scan clots of color
sprawled across grass, looking for the children
we pushed from our bodies
and gave up to this world.
Like chatty birds of prey
trading gossip and snacks, we squint
at distant field events, ready to translate
the announcer's squawk into a particular
first call. Fathers drift away
to pace, to film a start
or handoff, to coach the last turn.
It comes down to this: knots of mothers
trying to be casual about sport, trying
with our collective *juju* to ward off
injury, trying to maintain the ideal
of personal best, and wanting,
deep down, their baby to win.
And our sons! All bone and leg.
We become grim silence as they race away,
wanting to warn of the runner behind,
as if they did not know the ragged
breath on their shoulder from their own.
At this stage everything's metaphor: each step
increases the distance while we're reduced
to watching from bleachers. We want to let go.
We've been practicing too. And yet we know
how deep they can reach, how much beyond all
they can give. That rush of kick
still feels like ours.

About the Author

Candace Black was born in Fort Sill, Oklahoma, and spent most of her youth on U.S. Marine Corps bases in southern California. She received a B.A. in English from California State University, Chico, and a M.F.A. in Creative Writing from the University of Montana. Her work has been recognized by several grants, including a 1988 Loft-McKnight Award and a 1998 SASE/Jerome Foundation Fellowship. She lives in Mankato, Minnesota, with her husband, poet Richard Robbins, and their two sons.